The Design Container

Build the best environment for innovation and creativity

For

SaaS and Enterprise products
Product Design teams
Engineering teams
and Startups

By Abdalla Emam

indypixels.co | 2024

Introduction

The Imperative of a New Design Approach in Tech Companies and Startups

Many tech companies' current design processes and software frameworks are insufficient for delivering the value customers expect today. The recent economic downturn and layoffs have only exacerbated these shortcomings, highlighting the need for a fundamental shift toward a new design-first approach. This strategy is not just about aesthetics or usability; it's about creating products that resonate with users on a deeper level, fostering long-term engagement, and ensuring that businesses can adapt to the ever-changing demands of the tech market.

In today's rapidly evolving digital landscape, the need for a design-first approach in technology companies and startups has never been more critical. As competition intensifies and customer expectations continue to rise, businesses must differentiate themselves through products that not only function well but also deliver exceptional user experiences. However, many companies still rely on traditional development methodologies, prioritizing engineering or business objectives over design.

In fact, a report by the Design Management Institute revealed that design-driven companies outperformed the S&P 500 by 211% between 2005 and 2015, emphasizing the financial advantage of integrating design into every stage of the development process.

Tech companies face growing pressures to deliver faster and more cost-effective solutions, often at the expense of quality. As of late 2023, a significant number of major tech firms have implemented widespread layoffs, with the U.S. tech sector shedding more than 200,000 jobs since early 2022. These cuts, while aimed at reducing operational costs, have severely impacted product teams, particularly those focused on user experience and customer-centric roles.

Consequently, companies are left with leaner teams that must produce at a pace that sacrifices thoughtful design processes, leading to diminished product value and increased user frustration.

According to a 2023 study by McKinsey, customer satisfaction in digital products dropped by over 12% year-on-year, directly correlating with the reduction in resources dedicated to design and user research. This growing dissatisfaction highlights how critical it is to prioritize design from the outset to maintain user engagement and trust.

A design-first approach integrates design thinking into every phase of product development, ensuring that user experience is not an afterthought but the foundation upon which a product is built. This methodology aligns with the changing nature of consumer expectations, where seamless interaction, emotional engagement, and intuitive functionality are key drivers of brand loyalty. Companies that fail to prioritize these elements in their products are at risk of being outpaced by competitors who do. Despite this, the current processes in many tech firms and startups still treat design as an isolated phase rather than a continuous, iterative practice embedded within product strategy. The lack of a unified design process contributes to inefficiencies and missed opportunities for delivering more impactful user experiences.

One of the main reasons the current design processes and software frameworks fall short is their failure to adapt to the complexities of today's product ecosystems. Traditional models often separate design from development, creating silos that hinder collaboration and slow down innovation. Agile and lean methodologies, while successful in some areas, tend to prioritize speed and iteration over thorough design validation, leading to products that are technically functional but lack the refinement necessary for long-term success. This disconnect between design and execution means companies often release products misaligned with user needs, resulting in higher churn rates and lower adoption.

Additionally, the software frameworks commonly used today, such as Agile, often emphasize rapid prototyping and incremental improvements but lack the depth required for holistic design thinking. These frameworks are optimized for quick releases, but without embedding design principles deeply into their core, they risk producing products that fall short in terms of usability and overall user satisfaction. While speed to market is critical, especially in startups, sacrificing a thoughtful design process leads to products that fail to engage users at an emotional or practical level. This results in higher support costs, negative user reviews, and, ultimately, lost revenue.

As the tech landscape continues to evolve, customers are no longer just passive consumers; they have become more informed, discerning, and vocal about their expectations. Recent market data from the American Customer Satisfaction Index (ACSI) showed that satisfaction with technology products fell by 6% in 2023, a significant drop attributed to the rapid decline in product quality post-layoffs in major tech companies. The need for products that are easy to use, aesthetically pleasing, and responsive to customer feedback is more pressing than ever. In a marketplace saturated with options, users will quickly abandon products that do not meet their needs, and word of mouth, through online reviews and social media, can accelerate the downfall of poorly designed products.

Moreover, with artificial intelligence and automation reshaping the future of product development, design's role is becoming even more central. AI-driven tools are enabling faster and more efficient product iterations, but without human-centered design principles guiding their use, the technology alone will not be enough to meet user expectations.

In sum, companies that fail to adapt to a design-first approach risk falling behind in an era where user experience is the key differentiator. Incorporating AI into design processes will allow for greater customization and personalization, but these advancements must be guided by a deep understanding of user needs, which only a design-led framework can provide.

Chapter 1

The Design Container: An introduction to the framework

The design container is a framework that can help you build the best environment to design and develop SaaS Products, Enterprise tech startups, and software teams using a fusion of the following methodologies: **the container method, user-centered design**, and **mindfulness**.

Let's go into even more detail to help you fully understand how to build the best team and working environment for SaaS product development using **The Design Container Framework**. The goal here is to create a high-performing environment that fosters creativity, agility, and well-being, all while maintaining focus on delivering a product that serves users' needs effectively. I'll break each part down in more depth and show how to apply them in practical scenarios.

The **Design Container Framework** is also an effective method for managing complexity in SaaS product development, especially in tech startups where agility, creativity, and alignment are key to success.

The Design Container Framework:
Creating Structure for Freedom and Innovation

The core idea behind **the Design Container Framework** is to create **"containers"**—clearly defined safe spaces that foster innovation and creativity and guide teams through problem-solving or product development. These containers are designed to balance **autonomy** and **accountability**. Within these containers, teams have the **freedom to innovate** and experiment, but their work must align with broader organizational goals, strategic objectives, or user needs.

This structured approach avoids the chaos of having too much freedom while still allowing teams the creative space they need to innovate.

Let's break down the key components and how to apply them effectively.

The Design Container Framework can be divided into two main pillars: **the parameters of the design container,** which we'll discuss in this chapter, and **the process of the design container,** which we'll discuss in Chapter 6. Combined, they complete the framework and should be adapted and used in parlors.

Parameters of the Design Container Framework

1. **Clear Boundaries (The Container)**
2. **Autonomy Within the Container**
3. **Cross-Functional Collaboration**
4. **Iterative Cycles (Feedback Loops)**
5. **Review and Realignment (Continuous Learning)**

The container parameters

The design container framework
2024 © by Abdalla Emam
indypixel.co

1. Clear Boundaries (The Container)

The first step in the framework is to define the purpose and boundaries of the container clearly. This ensures that teams understand the goals they're working towards while still allowing them enough room to innovate within those boundaries.

What are the Boundaries?

Clear boundaries in the Design Container Framework refer to:

- **Goals**: What is the container trying to achieve? For example, "Create a seamless onboarding experience for new users within two months."
- **Scope**: What is included and what's not? This prevents scope creep and ensures that teams stay focused on what's important.
- **Resources**: Teams need to know what resources they have—people, time, tools, and budget.
- **Constraints**: Highlight any limitations, such as technical constraints, compliance issues, or deadlines, that the team must respect.

By setting these parameters, teams know what they can experiment with and where they need to align with organizational rules or broader product strategies.

How to Apply:

Create a Container for Each Feature or Problem Area: If you're developing a SaaS product, create different containers for major features, such as user authentication, reporting dashboards, or collaboration tools. For example, one container could be "improving customer retention through better email engagement tools."

Scenario

Let's say your SaaS platform handles project management for remote teams. You could define a container like:

Goal: Improve task management and tracking for remote team members.

Scope: Focus on the User Interface (UI) and User Experience (UX) for the task assignment and progress tracking features. Do not work on notifications or calendar integration yet.

Resources: 3 designers, 2 developers, 1 product manager, and access to user feedback data.

Constraints: It must be launched within three months and must follow existing brand and UX guidelines.

2. Autonomy Within the Container: Empower Teams to Innovate

Once the boundaries are set, the team is given **autonomy** within the container. They are free to explore, experiment, and innovate as long as they stay within the defined boundaries. This fosters a sense of ownership and allows team members to bring their best ideas forward without waiting for approvals on every small decision.

Why Autonomy Matters:

- **Empowerment**: Teams that are trusted to make their own decisions feel more motivated and engaged. They are more likely to take risks and come up with creative solutions.
- **Speed and Agility**: Decisions can be made quickly without bottlenecks, leading to faster iteration and learning.
- **Innovation**: Freedom within the framework encourages teams to explore unconventional approaches, test hypotheses, and innovate.

How to Apply:

- **Delegate Decision-Making Power**: Allow teams to make decisions regarding design, prototyping, and testing without needing constant approval from senior leadership.

- **Ownership of Solutions**: Give the team full responsibility for delivering the outcomes within their container. Let them choose which tools, technologies, and design methods they will use to meet the container's goals.

Scenario

In the project management SaaS, the team working on the "task management" container could decide to experiment with a Kanban-style interface. They can create quick prototypes and test them with users without needing extensive approvals as long as they stick to the defined goals.

3. Cross-Functional Collaboration: Creating Diverse, Interdisciplinary Teams

Each container should be filled with a **cross-functional team**. This is a group of people with complementary skills, such as designers, developers, product managers, and marketers, all working together toward the container's goals. Cross-functional collaboration ensures that different perspectives are considered during the problem-solving process.

Why Cross-Functional Teams Work:

- **Holistic Approach**: A problem can be solved from multiple angles, considering design, engineering, business, and user experience aspects all at once.
- **Break Down Silos**: Cross-functional teams avoid the bottlenecks and miscommunications that often occur when departments work in isolation.
- **Rapid Feedback**: Teams can rapidly iterate because they have all the necessary skills in one place to brainstorm, prototype, test, and implement solutions.

How to Apply:

- **Assemble the Right Mix of Skills**: Make sure each container has a balanced team with all the necessary expertise. For example, a container focused on UI improvements might include a UX designer, a front-end developer, a product manager, and a QA engineer.

- **Foster Collaboration**: Create an environment where team members are encouraged to collaborate and share ideas across disciplines. Use collaborative tools (e.g., Slack, Miro, Trello) and practices like daily stand-ups or weekly check-ins to keep everyone aligned.

> **Scenario:**
>
> In the task management container, you might have:
>
> o A UX designer focusing on how tasks are visually represented.
> o A front-end developer implementing the interface.
> o A product manager ensuring the features align with customer feedback.
> o A marketer considering how task management can be a selling point in-product messaging.

4. Iterative Cycles: Creating Feedback Loops for Continuous Improvement

Within each container, teams should operate in **iterative cycles**. This means that instead of working on one large release over several months, the team works in small sprints, where they deliver a version of the product, gather feedback, and then iterate based on what they've learned.

Why Iteration is Important:

• **Faster Learning**: Teams learn what works and what doesn't much faster by testing smaller increments of work. This minimizes the risk of wasting time on solutions that will fail.
• **User Feedback**: Iterative development means you can gather user feedback early and often. This ensures that the final product is closely aligned with user needs.
• **Flexibility**: The team can pivot and adjust its direction based on feedback, emerging trends, or new challenges.

How to Apply:

• **Set Short Iterations (Sprints)**: Use Agile or Lean methodologies to break work into sprints (e.g., 1-2 weeks). After each sprint, review progress, gather feedback, and adjust the next sprint based on what you learned.

- **Test Prototypes and Features Regularly**: Develop quick prototypes or Minimum Viable Products (MVPs) within the container and test them with real users or stakeholders at the end of each iteration.

Scenario

The task management team could spend a sprint building a prototype for a new way of organizing tasks, test it with 10 real users, gather feedback, and adjust the design based on user input before moving into further development.

5. Review and Realignment: Continuous Learning and Adjustment

The container's progress should be reviewed at **regular intervals** to ensure that the work aligns with broader business goals and customer needs. This is the time for reflection and realignment—where teams ask, "Are we still on track to meet our goals?" and adjust if necessary.

Why Realignment is Key:

- **Maintain Focus**: Regular reviews prevent teams from drifting too far away from the original container goals. They also help avoid wasted time on features or experiments that don't align with user or business needs.
- **Adapt to Change**: As startups and SaaS products evolve rapidly, business priorities, customer feedback, or market conditions can change. Regular review meetings ensure teams can adapt to those changes without losing momentum.
- **Capture Learnings**: Reflection allows teams to capture what they've learned from failed experiments or successful prototypes and apply those lessons to future cycles.

How to Apply:

- **Hold Regular Review Sessions**: Every few weeks or at the end of each sprint, hold a review session where the team presents its progress. Review goals, check for alignment, and adjust the container if new information or challenges have emerged.
- **Be Open to Pivoting**: If the team finds that an experiment didn't work, they should have the freedom to pivot and try a new approach. The container boundaries should be flexible enough to allow for these changes.

Scenario

After a sprint, the task management team realizes that the new Kanban-style task organization isn't resonating with users. In the review, they decide to pivot and try a different approach, like a list-based task manager with advanced filtering options.

Benefits of the Design Container Framework

1. Fosters Innovation: The framework encourages creativity and experimentation by giving teams the freedom to explore within clear boundaries.

Promotes Agility: Teams can move quickly, testing and iterating.

Chapter 2

User-Centered Design (UCD): Keeping the User at the Heart of Product Development

User-centered design (UCD) is a design process that prioritizes the **needs, goals, and pain points of users** at every stage of product development. Whether you're building a SaaS product, an app, or a website, UCD ensures that the final product aligns with the real-world problems and desires of the people who will use it. By continuously engaging users, gathering feedback, and iterating based on that input, UCD ensures a product that not only works but is intuitive, valuable, and loved by its target audience.

Let's dive deep into the **philosophy, key principles**, and **step-by-step process** of UCD, with detailed examples and strategies for effectively applying it in a SaaS development environment.

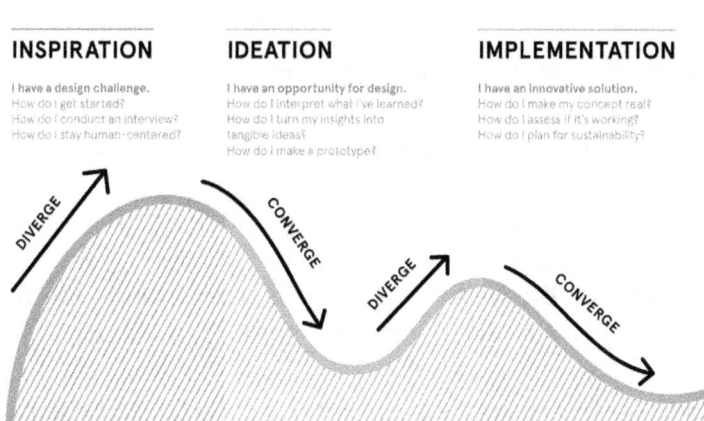

UCD Approach by IDEO - Illustration by Juan Fernando Pacheco

Core Philosophy of UCD

The central tenet of UCD is **empathy**—putting yourself in the user's shoes to truly understand their needs. In the SaaS industry, this means focusing not just on functionality but on the **user's experience**, whether it's ease of use, reducing friction, or making interactions more enjoyable.

The essence of UCD revolves around several key ideas:

- **Involve users early and often** in the design process.
- **Design for real users**, not assumptions about what they need.
- **Iterate based on user feedback** and continually refine the product.
- **Balance business needs with user needs**—both must coexist harmoniously for a product to succeed.

Key Principles of User-Centered Design

1. **Understand Your Users**
2. **Focus on Usability**
3. **Design for Real Scenarios**
4. **Iterative Testing and Improvement**
5. **Incorporate Feedback Loops**
6. **Accessibility and Inclusivity**

1. Understanding Your Users

The first and most critical step in UCD is understanding who your users are. This means developing a deep understanding of their goals, behaviors, motivations, and pain points through research. It's about knowing not only what users want to achieve but also how they think and behave when interacting with technology.

How to Apply:

• **User Research**: Conduct interviews, surveys, or ethnographic research to gather insights about your target audience. In SaaS development, this could involve talking to customers, observing how they use existing tools, and identifying where frustrations arise.

• **Develop User Personas**: Based on your research, create detailed personas that represent your core user groups. These personas help guide design decisions by ensuring that your team is always thinking about specific, real users instead of abstract concepts.

> **Scenario**
>
> For a SaaS project management tool, user research might reveal that small business owners need simplicity and automation, while enterprise project managers require more robust analytics and reporting tools. You would then create different personas to represent these users—each with distinct needs that guide design decisions.

2. Focus on Usability

Usability is at the core of UCD. A usable product is one that users can understand quickly and interact with easily without needing extensive training or support. This requires focusing on clarity, simplicity, and efficiency in design.

How to Apply:

- **Simplicity Over Complexity**: Focus on designing intuitive interfaces that allow users to accomplish tasks with minimal steps. Complex features should not overwhelm users.
- **Consistent Design Patterns**: Use consistent navigation and interaction patterns throughout the product so users don't have to relearn how to use different parts of the tool.
- **Clear, Visible Feedback**: Ensure that the product gives users immediate, clear feedback when they perform an action (e.g., a success message after saving a document or an error alert when something goes wrong).

> **Scenario**
>
> When designing the task management dashboard for your SaaS platform, you might emphasize easy-to-understand drag-and-drop functionality. Clear buttons, a minimalist interface, and visible confirmation when a task is assigned ensure that users feel in control and confident in their actions.

3. Design for Real Scenarios

Your product should solve real problems that users face. By understanding user workflows and designing around them, you ensure that your SaaS product becomes an integral part of their day-to-day tasks.

How to Apply:

• **Task-Based Design**: Map out common user tasks and ensure your design makes these tasks easy to accomplish. Think about what steps a user takes to achieve a goal, and design your interface to support those steps logically and smoothly.

• **User Flows**: Create user flow diagrams to understand the steps users take within your system. This helps eliminate unnecessary steps or friction points when completing their tasks.

Scenario

Imagine you're developing a feature for scheduling tasks in a SaaS project management tool. A common scenario might involve a project manager assigning tasks, checking dependencies, and reviewing progress. Your design should facilitate these actions without requiring the user to jump through multiple confusing steps.

4. Iterative Testing and Improvement

At the heart of UCD is the idea of **continuous improvement**. This means you don't build the entire product in one go. Instead, you build, test, gather feedback, and improve iteratively. The feedback loop is crucial—each version of your product is an improvement based on real user input.

How to Apply:

- **Low-Fidelity Prototypes**: Start by creating low-fidelity wireframes or prototypes. These can be simple sketches or clickable mockups that focus on structure and layout rather than detailed design.
- **User Testing**: Present these prototypes to actual users and observe how they interact with the system. Capture their feedback on usability, functionality, and pain points. Testing early versions ensures that major usability issues are identified and fixed before significant development resources are committed.
- **Iterate and Refine**: After each round of feedback, refine the design and build the next version. This cycle continues throughout the development process, ensuring that the product evolves based on user insights.

> **Scenario**
>
> You could create a clickable wireframe of a new reporting dashboard for your SaaS platform and test it with a group of users (e.g., project managers). They might point out that certain metrics are difficult to find, or that the layout feels cluttered. Based on their feedback, you would refine the layout, simplify the navigation, and present a new version for further testing.

5. Incorporate Feedback Loops

UCD is not a one-time activity; it's a continuous process. Even after the product is launched, feedback from users should be constantly gathered, analyzed, and used to improve the product.

How to Apply:

• **In-Product Feedback Mechanisms**: Provide users with an easy way to give feedback on the product, such as through surveys, feedback buttons, or direct support channels.

• **Analytics and User Behavior**: Track how users interact with your SaaS product using tools like heatmaps or usage analytics. This data provides insights into where users encounter difficulties or which features are most/least used.

• **Customer Interviews and Support Channels**: Regularly conduct post-launch interviews or gather feedback from customer support teams to understand what's working and what needs improvement.

> **Scenario**
>
> If you find that users are struggling to use a specific feature (e.g., task dependencies in a project management tool), you can prioritize improvements to that feature in your product roadmap. Continuous updates based on real-world user data keep your product relevant and user-friendly.

6. Accessibility and Inclusivity

A key aspect of UCD is designing products that are accessible to as many users as possible. This involves thinking about users with different abilities, preferences, and technological access. Accessibility ensures that your product can be used by people with disabilities, and inclusivity makes sure no one is left out due to design biases or assumptions.

How to Apply:

• **Accessible Design**: Follow accessibility standards such as the Web Content Accessibility Guidelines (WCAG). This includes designing for screen readers, offering keyboard navigation, and ensuring sufficient color contrast.

• **Responsive and Inclusive Design**: Design for users on a range of devices (mobile, tablet, desktop) and from different cultural or linguistic backgrounds. Avoid making assumptions about users' preferences or access to technology.

• **Test with Diverse User Groups**: Make sure your user testing includes individuals with disabilities or those who use assistive technologies to catch accessibility issues early.

Scenario

For your SaaS platform, you ensure that all icons have accompanying text for screen readers, forms are fully navigable via keyboard, and that color contrast passes WCAG standards. You also design the user interface to be mobile-responsive, as many project managers might check tasks or schedules on their phones.

Step-by-Step Process of User-Centered Design

Here's a more detailed breakdown of how to apply UCD in a SaaS product development environment:

1. Research and Discovery

This stage involves gathering as much information as possible about your users. You need to discover who they are, what they need, and what their pain points are.

- **Methods**: Surveys, interviews, user observations, focus groups, competitive analysis.
- **Output**: User personas, user stories, problem definitions.

2. Define the Problem and Goals

Based on your research, clearly define the problem your SaaS product or feature aims to solve. It's important that this problem is rooted in user needs, not assumptions.

- **Methods**: Synthesis of research, creating user journeys, story mapping.
- **Output**: Problem statements, project goals.

3. Ideation

Now that the problem is defined, brainstorm possible solutions. The key here is to think widely and creatively, coming up with as many ideas as possible without judgment.

- **Methods**: Brainstorming sessions, sketching, mind mapping.
- **Output**: Initial design concepts, rough sketches.

4. Prototyping

Create tangible representations of your ideas, either as paper prototypes, wireframes, or clickable mockups. These prototypes should be basic at first, focusing on structure rather than details.

- **Methods**: Wireframes, low-fidelity prototypes.
- **Output**: Prototypes ready for user testing.

5. User Testing

Test the prototypes with real users. The goal is to understand how they interact with the design, what works, and what causes confusion.

- **Methods**: Usability testing, A/B testing, card sorting.
- **Output**: Feedback, usability reports, design adjustments.

6. Iteration

Based on user feedback, refine the design and build another iteration. This cycle continues until the product is intuitive, functional, and meets user needs.

- **Methods**: Design iteration, development sprints.
- **Output**: Improved prototypes and eventually a fully developed feature/product.

7. Launch and Post-Launch Feedback

Once the product is launched, continue gathering feedback through analytics, support tickets, and direct user feedback to guide future improvements.

- **Methods**: User analytics, in-product surveys, and user interviews.
- **Output**: Roadmap updates, ongoing improvements.

Benefits of UCD

1. Higher User Satisfaction: Products developed with UCD are more likely to meet the actual needs of users, leading to higher satisfaction and loyalty.

2. Reduced Development Costs: Identifying usability problems early in the process reduces costly changes later in development.

3. Fewer Support Requests: When a product is easy to use and intuitive, users are less likely to need support, reducing the load on customer service teams.

4. Improved Product Adoption: Products that align with user needs and are easy to use see higher adoption rates and lower churn in SaaS environments.

User-Centered Design is an iterative process that places the user at the heart of product development. By understanding user needs, focusing on usability, and continually iterating based on feedback, you ensure that the final product is not only functional but also meaningful and valuable. In the fast-paced world of SaaS, UCD ensures that your product evolves in line with user expectations, leading to greater success in the market.

Challenges with the UCD approach

A user-centered design (UCD) approach, while essential for creating products that resonate with users, cannot by itself guarantee a perfect framework for building a digital product or establishing healthy boundaries in a tech team. UCD primarily focuses on the end user, but product development also requires balancing technical constraints, business goals, and team dynamics. Without addressing these aspects, focusing solely on user needs can result in unrealistic expectations, technical debt, or misaligned priorities. In team settings, UCD alone doesn't provide a framework for setting clear roles, and responsibilities, or managing workload. Healthy boundaries within a tech team come from leadership, communication, and mutual respect, ensuring that both user-focused goals and the team's well-being are prioritized.

Chapter 3

Uniting Forces: How Design Thinking Complements User-Centered Design for Innovation and Impact

In the world of product development, and specifically in tech startups, both **User-Centered Design (UCD)** and **Design Thinking** have emerged as powerful methodologies for solving complex problems, creating user-focused products, and fostering innovation. While they are often discussed separately, these two frameworks are deeply complementary. When integrated thoughtfully, UCD and Design Thinking amplify each other's strengths, enabling teams to create more meaningful, innovative, and user-driven solutions. This chapter explores how User-Centered Design can be enhanced and complemented by Design Thinking strategies to build better products that solve real-world problems effectively and creatively.

Introducing Design Thinking: A Framework for Creative Problem Solving

Design Thinking is a human-centered approach to innovation that emphasizes empathy, creativity, and iteration. Unlike UCD, which follows a more structured approach, Design Thinking encourages teams to think outside the box, embrace ambiguity, and explore diverse solutions.

The Design Thinking process typically includes five stages:

1. **Empathize**: Understand the users by stepping into their shoes, using ethnographic research methods to gain deep insights into their needs and pain points.

2. **Define**: Frame the problem by synthesizing research insights into a clear, actionable problem statement.

3. **Ideate**: Brainstorm a wide range of potential solutions, focusing on quantity and creativity rather than feasibility in this phase.

4. **Prototype**: Build low-fidelity prototypes that can be quickly tested and iterated upon.

5. **Test**: Engage users in testing the prototypes gathering feedback to refine and improve the solutions iteratively.

Unlike UCD, which often focuses on refining solutions based on well-defined problems, Design Thinking fosters creativity by encouraging divergent thinking (generating many potential solutions) followed by convergent thinking (narrowing down to the most viable options). It's a more flexible, fluid process, encouraging teams to challenge assumptions and explore innovative solutions that might not have been obvious initially.

Design Thinking

Empathize   Define   Ideate   Prototype   Test

Interaction Design Foundation
interaction-design.org

How UCD and Design Thinking Complement Each Other

Though User-Centered Design and Design Thinking share a common goal of creating human-centered products, their methodologies offer unique strengths that can complement one another. While UCD ensures that the end product is usable and tailored to real users' needs, Design Thinking adds a layer of creativity, allowing for innovation and out-of-the-box thinking.

Below, we explore the specific ways UCD and Design Thinking can enhance each other:

1. Broadening the Scope of Problem Framing: Moving Beyond Immediate User Needs

User-Centered Design typically starts by identifying **specific problems** that users face. While this ensures the design process is grounded in real-world pain points, it can sometimes lead to solutions that focus too much on **incremental improvements** rather than disruptive innovation. UCD can lead teams to concentrate solely on refining existing processes or interfaces, without necessarily rethinking the problem from a broader perspective.

How Design Thinking Helps:

- Design Thinking expands the problem-framing stage by focusing on **empathizing** with users in a deeper, more holistic way. It asks teams not only to identify existing pain points but also to challenge assumptions about the problem itself. The **Define** phase of Design Thinking encourages teams to rethink the nature of the user's problem and ask questions like, "Are we solving the right problem?" or "Is there a bigger underlying issue we're missing?"
- By combining UCD's research-driven insights with Design Thinking's **reframing** strategies, teams can uncover **opportunities for innovation** that might otherwise be overlooked.

Scenario

Imagine a team working on a mobile app for banking. UCD might focus on making the user interface more intuitive or improving the flow of transactions. However, by applying Design Thinking strategies, the team might zoom out and ask, "Why do users need to engage in so many transactions? Can we reduce their need to interact with the app altogether by automating certain processes?" This shift in perspective opens the door for more radical innovation.

2. Fueling Creativity in the Ideation Phase

One limitation of User-Centered Design is that it often gravitates toward **incremental improvements** rather than radical innovations. Because UCD focuses so much on user feedback and usability testing, teams can become overly reliant on what users say they want rather than exploring creative solutions that users might not even be aware of.

How Design Thinking Helps:

- Design Thinking's **Ideation** phase encourages teams to generate a wide variety of ideas, including unconventional and bold ones. By combining this creative freedom with UCD's structured approach to user needs, teams can push beyond incremental changes and explore more transformative ideas.
- Design Thinking's focus on **divergent thinking**—generating as many ideas as possible without filtering them based on feasibility—gives teams the freedom to experiment with wild ideas. Once the ideation phase is complete, UCD principles can be used to evaluate and refine the ideas, ensuring that the solutions still meet real user needs.

Scenario

A healthcare company might use UCD to improve the user interface of a patient portal, making it easier for patients to schedule appointments or access medical records. However, by introducing Design Thinking's ideation techniques, the team might start asking broader questions: "What if we could eliminate the need for a patient portal altogether? Could we develop a voice-activated system that allows patients to schedule appointments through smart speakers?" This approach leads to more creative solutions while still ensuring usability.

3. Encouraging Iteration and Learning Through Prototyping

UCD focuses heavily on **testing** and **iteration**. Once a solution is designed, teams prototype and gather feedback, then refine the solution based on usability tests. However, because UCD often centers around **incremental** improvements, teams might focus on optimizing specific features rather than exploring completely new concepts.

How Design Thinking Helps:

- Design Thinking embraces **rapid prototyping** of many different ideas early in the process. Rather than perfecting one solution, Design Thinking encourages teams to build multiple low-fidelity prototypes and test them quickly, allowing for rapid experimentation and learning.
- By pairing UCD's iterative testing with Design Thinking's focus on **multiple rounds of ideation and prototyping**, teams can iterate not just on the refinement of a single solution but on the exploration of entirely different solutions.

Scenario

A company developing an AI-powered chatbot for customer service might follow UCD to fine-tune the chatbot's responses based on user feedback. However, by using design thinking, the team might prototype multiple chatbot interfaces or explore entirely different interaction models, such as voice assistants, to see which users prefer. This process of iterative prototyping allows for greater creativity and user validation.

4. Integrating User Insights Throughout the Process

One of UCD's key strengths is its focus on continuously involving users throughout the development process. By gathering user feedback through research, personas, and usability testing, UCD ensures that design decisions are always grounded in user needs.

How Design Thinking Helps:

- While UCD emphasizes **evaluative research** (i.e., testing solutions with users), Design Thinking brings in a stronger focus on **exploratory research** during the **Empathize** phase. This deeper, qualitative research not only helps uncover user needs but also reveals latent desires and problems users might not explicitly articulate.
- Design Thinking's approach to **empathy-driven research** helps teams better understand the emotional, cultural, and psychological contexts of users, allowing for a more profound understanding of user behavior. By integrating these insights into UCD's iterative testing process, teams can ensure that the final product resonates with users on both a practical and emotional level.

> **Scenario**
>
> A fitness app might use UCD to ensure that the interface is easy to navigate, with features that align with user preferences. However, by applying Design Thinking's empathy research, the team might discover deeper insights into users' motivations for fitness, such as a desire for community or stress relief. This insight could lead to the development of features that go beyond usability, such as social challenges or mental wellness content.

5. Leveraging Divergent and Convergent Thinking for Innovation

One of the core tensions in design is balancing **creativity** (divergent thinking) with **practicality** (convergent thinking). UCD, with its focus on user needs and testing, naturally leans toward convergent thinking—finding practical solutions that address clear problems. Design Thinking, however, emphasizes the balance between divergent thinking (generating many ideas) and convergent thinking (selecting and refining the best ideas).

How Design Thinking Helps:

- By incorporating Design Thinking's focus on **divergent thinking** during the ideation phase, UCD teams can explore more creative and varied solutions before narrowing down to the most feasible ones. This helps break the tendency of UCD processes to result in **incremental changes** rather than **transformative innovations**.

Scenario

A team working on a travel booking platform might use UCD to optimize the booking flow, improving usability by making incremental changes. By adding Design Thinking into the mix, the team might also brainstorm bold new ideas—like integrating virtual reality for destination exploration or personalizing recommendations based on mood. This process allows the team to explore both practical and innovative solutions, ensuring a final product that is both usable and forward-thinking.

A Synergistic Approach for Human-Centered Innovation

When combined, User-Centered Design and Design Thinking provide a powerful framework for creating **human-centered, innovative products**. UCD ensures that the product meets the needs of real users through research, testing, and iterative refinement. Meanwhile, Design Thinking injects creativity, encourages bold solutions, and embraces experimentation, pushing teams to explore opportunities beyond the immediate problem.

By leveraging the complementary strengths of both methodologies, teams can design products that not only solve user problems effectively but also delight and inspire. This synergistic approach is particularly valuable in today's fast-paced, ever-evolving landscape, where companies must continually innovate while remaining deeply attuned to their users' needs.

In essence, the **fusion** of User-Centered Design and Design Thinking leads to **smarter, more creative, and more impactful solutions**—the perfect recipe for success in today's competitive market.

Chapter 4

The Scrum Trap: How Rigid Processes Can Hinder Creativity and Innovation

In today's fast-paced and competitive business world, Scrum has become one of the most widely adopted project management frameworks for software development and beyond. Its emphasis on short development cycles, daily standups, and close team collaboration has made it an attractive solution for companies seeking agility. However, despite its benefits in organizing workflows and improving efficiency, Scrum can inadvertently stifle creativity and innovation. In this chapter, we will explore how the very principles that make Scrum so appealing in managing tasks and meeting deadlines can sometimes act as constraints, limiting the creative and exploratory processes that fuel innovation within companies.

Understanding Scrum: A Process Designed for Efficiency

Scrum is an agile framework designed to break down large projects into manageable chunks of work, typically called **sprints**. Each sprint is typically a 2-4 week cycle in which a cross-functional team works to deliver a **shippable product increment**. Key elements of Scrum include:

- **Daily Standups**: Short meetings where team members discuss progress, blockers, and next steps.
- **Sprint Planning**: Meetings where the team selects work for the upcoming sprint from the **product backlog**.
- **Retrospectives**: Post-sprint discussions where teams evaluate what went well, what didn't, and how they can improve.
- **Fixed Timelines**: Each sprint operates within a fixed timeframe, ensuring predictability and a clear focus on deliverables.

While Scrum is celebrated for keeping projects organized, on track, and transparent, its structured nature can be at odds with the less predictable and often chaotic process of innovation. Let's dive into some of the reasons why.

1. Overemphasis on Short-Term Goals Hinders Long-Term Vision

In Scrum, the team's focus is typically on completing the work agreed upon for a given sprint. Each sprint is driven by **user stories**, which describe specific features or tasks that need to be developed. This sprint-by-sprint approach often prioritizes delivering on immediate goals rather than fostering the kind of long-term thinking that innovation requires.

Impact on Creativity:

- **Narrow Focus:** The constant pressure to deliver within a sprint means teams are incentivized to focus on what is immediately achievable rather than stepping back and exploring new, potentially disruptive ideas. Time-intensive exploration, experimentation, and research—key drivers of innovation—often get sidelined in favor of incremental improvements.
- **Reactive Development**: Teams may spend more time reacting to immediate user feedback and backlog requirements than proactively exploring future-oriented solutions or creative ways to rethink the product entirely.

Limitation Example

Imagine a team tasked with improving an e-commerce platform's checkout process. In a Scrum framework, they might be focused on implementing quick fixes such as improving the loading time or adding new payment options to meet sprint goals. However, the sprint cadence leaves little room for deeper, more creative questions like, "What if the checkout experience could be reimagined entirely?" or "Could AI eliminate the checkout process altogether?" Instead, the focus remains on incremental updates rather than breakthrough innovations.

2. Rigidity in Timeboxing and Fixed Sprints Limits Experimentation

Innovation thrives on experimentation. When exploring new ideas, teams often need the freedom to iterate and fail multiple times before arriving at a breakthrough solution. In Scrum, the practice of **timeboxing**—setting strict deadlines for completing tasks within a sprint—can work against this exploratory nature.

Impact on Creativity:

- **Pressure to Ship**: The strict sprint timelines create an urgency to "ship" something tangible at the end of each cycle, even if the solution hasn't been fully explored. This can encourage teams to choose safer, more reliable paths rather than experimenting with bold, creative ideas that may require longer development periods or risk failing.
- **Disincentive for Failure**: Experimentation and failure are essential for creativity, but Scrum's structure often rewards predictable progress over open-ended exploration. If the team fails to deliver a working feature within the sprint, it is seen as a failure. In contrast, in an innovation-centric environment, failure is often a learning opportunity. This mindset shift can be difficult to achieve within Scrum's strict deadlines.

Limitation Example

Consider a startup developing a new mobile app feature based on augmented reality (AR). The technology requires extensive research, testing, and iteration to get right. In a Scrum environment, the team may feel pressure to push out a basic, minimally viable version of the feature within a sprint rather than taking the time to fully explore its potential, resulting in a product that feels rushed and lacks innovation.

3. Focus on Deliverables Stifles Open-Ended Exploration

Scrum's success is often measured in terms of **deliverables**: each sprint ends with something tangible that can be demonstrated, tested, or shipped. This focus on delivering specific features or updates can overshadow more open-ended, discovery-driven exploration. In a creative, innovative process, the outcome is often unknown at the outset, and the most valuable breakthroughs are sometimes discovered serendipitously.

Impact on Creativity:

- **Output vs. Discovery**: Scrum prioritizes shipping concrete features at the end of each sprint, which can force teams to focus on outcomes they can clearly define upfront. This clashes with the nature of innovation, where the process itself—exploring the unknown, engaging in deep research, and considering unexpected insights—often leads to the most groundbreaking ideas.
- **Creativity Requires Ambiguity**: Scrum's need for a clear backlog of tasks doesn't easily accommodate the kind of open-ended, ambiguous work required for creativity. Teams are expected to break down work into digestible, well-defined user stories. This structure can limit opportunities for blue-sky thinking or speculative design, both of which often lead to novel and disruptive innovations.

Limitation Example

A tech company exploring how blockchain technology could revolutionize supply chain logistics might find that Scrum's emphasis on sprint deliverables stifles their efforts. The team may feel pressured to produce incremental features (e.g., adding blockchain to one part of the system) instead of devoting time to fully reimagining what a blockchain-driven supply chain could look like in the long term.

4. Scrum's Predictability Undermines the Messiness of Innovation

One of the biggest draws of Scrum is its predictability—each sprint follows a well-defined process, from **planning** to **execution** to **retrospective**. While this can enhance efficiency and ensure transparency, it can also undermine the inherent messiness of the innovation process.

Impact on Creativity:

- **Creativity Thrives in Uncertainty**: True innovation often requires venturing into uncharted territory where the outcome is uncertain. However, Scrum's predictability can make it difficult to navigate the ambiguity that drives creativity. Teams can become overly focused on executing tasks efficiently rather than questioning assumptions or experimenting with radical new approaches.
- **Reduced Risk-Taking**: Scrum's focus on predictability can discourage teams from taking risks. If a team knows that it must deliver something tangible by the end of the sprint, they are more likely to stick to the safe, tried-and-tested methods that they know will work rather than venturing into riskier, more innovative territory where failure is a possibility.

Limitation Example:

A design team tasked with developing a new user interface might, within the Scrum process, focus on making incremental changes like adjusting colors or rearranging UI elements to meet sprint goals. However, creativity in design often requires questioning the entire user experience and taking bold risks. Without the flexibility to engage in speculative design, teams may miss out on opportunities to deliver truly transformative experiences.

5. Daily Standups Can Foster Short-Term Thinking

Daily standup meetings are designed to keep the team on track by allowing each member to report on their progress, blockers, and next steps. While these meetings are useful for accountability, they can foster a myopic, short-term focus where teams become overly concerned with what was accomplished yesterday and what will be done today rather than stepping back to think about the big picture.

Impact on Creativity:

- **Short-Termism**: Daily standups can inadvertently lead to short-term thinking, where the focus is on the immediate progress being made toward sprint goals rather than fostering a broader vision. This constant need to demonstrate incremental progress can lead teams to shy away from creative exploration, which often takes longer and may not yield tangible results in the short term.
- **Pressure to Perform**: The public nature of daily standups, where each team member reports their progress, can create pressure to show constant productivity. This can result in a "heads-down" mentality where members are less willing to take creative risks, as they feel obligated to report consistent deliverables.

Limitation Example:

A software development team working on a complex algorithm might focus on small, easily reportable tasks during daily standups—such as optimizing performance or fixing bugs—rather than taking time to engage in deeper, more creative problem-solving. This limits opportunities for breakthrough innovations, as team members prioritize small, measurable wins over big-picture thinking.

Balancing Scrum with Creativity and Innovation

While Scrum offers a valuable framework for managing tasks and improving efficiency, it is essential to recognize its limitations when it comes to fostering creativity and innovation. Scrum's focus on short-term goals, timeboxed sprints, and deliverable-driven processes can conflict with the open-ended, exploratory, and often unpredictable nature of innovation.

To mitigate these challenges, companies must balance the structure of Scrum with opportunities for creative exploration. This might mean setting aside dedicated time for innovation outside the sprint cycles, encouraging risk-taking and experimentation, or even adopting alternative frameworks that complement Scrum's strengths with more room for creative freedom.

Ultimately, the key to driving innovation lies in creating an environment that values both **efficiency** and **exploration**. By loosening the constraints of Scrum where necessary and allowing teams to step back, explore, and take risks, companies can unlock their creative potential while still benefiting from the organizational power of agile methodologies.

Chapter 5

Mindfulness:
Building a Resilient, Focused Team Culture

Mindfulness is the practice of being fully present in the moment aware of your thoughts, emotions, and environment without judgment. Mindfulness helps build a culture of focus, emotional resilience, and enhanced collaboration when applied to the workplace. It encourages team members to stay present and manage their emotions, ultimately fostering a healthier, more balanced, and productive work environment. In the high-pressure world of SaaS product development and tech startups, these qualities are essential for sustaining creativity, reducing burnout, and encouraging innovative thinking.

What is Mindfulness in the Workplace?

In a mindful work environment, team members are encouraged to stay connected to the present moment, increasing their awareness of thoughts, feelings, and physical sensations. This heightened awareness leads to better emotional regulation, improved collaboration, and greater productivity. When employees practice mindfulness, they develop the ability to **focus** on tasks more effectively, manage **stress** proactively, and communicate with **greater clarity and empathy**.

The goal is to create a work culture where individuals feel empowered to bring their best selves to their work and maintain **clarity of thought** even in stressful situations.

Key Elements of Mindfulness in a Team Culture

1. **Mindful Work Practices**
2. **Emotional Intelligence**
3. **Work-Life Balance**
4. **Mindful Communication**
5. **Focus and Deep Work**

1. Mindful work practices

Mindful work practices are techniques that integrate mindfulness into the daily workflow, helping employees to stay grounded and present. These practices can range from short mindfulness exercises to long-term habits that build focus and mental clarity.

How to Implement Mindful Work Practices:

- **Mindful Breaks**: Introduce mindful breaks during the workday, workshops, and team meetings where team members step away from their tasks to focus on their breathing or engage in short meditations. This helps to **reset focus** and **reduce stress**.
- **Breathing Techniques**: Encourage simple breathing exercises, especially before important meetings or after stressful interactions, to calm the mind and regain composure.
- **Mindful Transitions**: Encourage mindful transitions between tasks by taking a brief moment to refocus before jumping into the next activity. This prevents overwhelm and helps the brain refocus.

Exercise

A SaaS team working through intense product sprints might incorporate a short **5-minute mindfulness break** every few hours to help employees reset. This could involve breathing exercises or simply stepping away from their screens to sit in silence. These practices ensure that the team remains **energized and focused** throughout the day.

2. Emotional Intelligence: Developing Self-Awareness and Empathy

Emotional intelligence (EQ) is the ability to recognize, understand, and manage your own emotions, as well as those of others. Mindfulness directly enhances EQ by helping employees become more aware of their emotional states and reactions. High EQ leads to **better team collaboration**, improved conflict resolution, and greater empathy within teams.

How to Foster Emotional Intelligence:

• **Self-Reflection Exercises**: Encourage team members to reflect on their emotions and identify patterns of stress, frustration, or excitement. This self-awareness can lead to better self-regulation and decision-making.
• **Empathy Training**: Incorporate mindfulness exercises that enhance empathy, such as **compassionate listening** or reflecting on how actions impact others.
• **Constructive Conflict Resolution**: Train teams to handle conflicts mindfully, using a calm, non-reactive approach to problem-solving and resolution.

In a high-stakes environment like a SaaS product launch, teams might experience friction due to tight deadlines. Leaders can use **mindful conflict resolution** techniques, encouraging team members to pause and reflect on their emotions before addressing the issue.

This reduces emotional reactivity and fosters collaborative problem-solving.

3. Work-Life Balance: Preventing Burnout and Fostering Creativity

Work-life balance is critical in maintaining **creativity** and **long-term productivity**. A mindful work culture recognizes the importance of rest and ensures that team members are not overworked or burned out. When employees feel recharged, they can approach their tasks with greater creativity and focus.

How to Promote Work-Life Balance:

- **Flexible Work Policies**: Offer flexible working hours or remote work options to help employees manage their personal and professional lives effectively.
- **"No-Meeting" Days**: Designate specific days of the week where no meetings are scheduled, allowing team members to focus on deep, uninterrupted work.
- **Encourage Time Off**: Foster a culture where taking regular time off is not only accepted but encouraged. Leaders should model this behavior by also taking time off to recharge.

Exercise

In a SaaS startup that operates in a fast-paced, high-pressure environment, the company might implement **"no-meeting Fridays"**, allowing the team to focus on creative problem-solving or coding without the pressure of back-to-back meetings. This promotes mental clarity and helps avoid burnout.

4. Mindful Communication: Fostering Open, Non-Judgmental Dialogue

Mindful communication encourages team members to communicate with empathy and clarity. It involves deep listening, being fully present in conversations, and responding thoughtfully. This type of communication enhances trust within the team, reduces misunderstandings, and improves overall collaboration.

How to Implement Mindful Communication:

- **Active Listening**: Train team members to engage in active listening, where they focus entirely on the speaker without thinking ahead to their response. This improves understanding and reduces miscommunication.
- **Non-Judgmental Feedback**: Encourage a culture of open feedback where ideas and concerns are expressed without fear of judgment. Focus feedback on behaviors and outcomes, not personal judgments.
- **Empathetic Responses**: Encourage team members to acknowledge and validate others' emotions before responding to challenges or disagreements. This fosters a supportive and trusting environment.

Exercise

In a product development meeting, a team member voices concerns about a particular feature design. Rather than dismissing or debating the concern, the team lead engages in **mindful listening**, reflecting on the feedback before responding. This approach encourages constructive discussions and promotes a culture of **psychological safety** where all ideas are valued.

5. Focus and Deep Work: Enhancing Productivity and Creativity

Mindfulness can significantly improve focus by training individuals to stay present and avoid distractions. For SaaS teams, where complex problem-solving and creativity are key, practicing mindfulness supports the ability to engage in **deep work**, where individuals can work for extended periods without distractions.

How to Promote Focus and Deep Work:

• **Time Blocking**: Implement time-blocking practices where team members dedicate specific hours to deep, focused work without interruptions.

• **Digital Detox**: Encourage team members to limit their exposure to distractions, such as unnecessary notifications or constant email checking, during deep work periods.

• **Mindful Transition Between Tasks**: Encourage employees to take short, mindful pauses when switching between tasks. This allows them to reset and approach the next task with full attention.

Exercise

A product manager at a SaaS company might schedule 2-hour blocks of **deep work** for feature development, turning off Slack notifications and emails during this period. This helps maintain a state of **flow**, increasing productivity and the quality of work produced.

Mindfulness in the workplace is more than just a trend; it's a proven approach to fostering **focus**, **creativity**, and **emotional intelligence**.

In SaaS environments where speed, innovation, and teamwork are critical, integrating mindfulness practices can lead to more **resilient teams**, improved **work-life balance**, and **enhanced product development**.

By staying present and aware, teams can navigate challenges with clarity, remain adaptable, and ultimately create a work environment where both individuals and the organization can thrive.

Chapter 6

The Complete Design Container Framework:
Parameters + Process

So, let's bring it all together! To simplify it further, we're going to reframe the integration of all the previous methods we have discussed so far under the three-phase process of the Design Container framework—**Explore**, **Define**, and **Evaluate**. These three-phase design processes are confined and limited within the framework parameters we discussed in Chapter One. This framework provides a structured yet flexible approach for SaaS product design and development, which we call **the design container framework**. Each of the steps has to cover each of the framework's main methods. This holistic framework aligns with the dynamic needs of tech startups, focusing on innovation, user satisfaction, and team well-being.

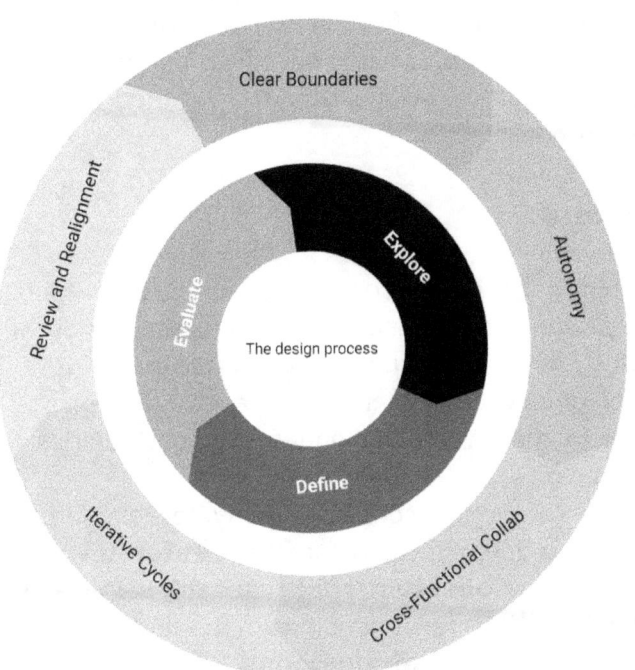

The complete design container framework
2024 © by Abdalla Emam
indypixel.co

Phase 1: Explore: Laying the Foundation

This phase is about understanding user needs, uncovering pain points, and defining the scope for each container. It's crucial for creating cross-functional teams that are focused on solving specific problems within their respective domains while remaining aligned with the larger product goals.

Actions:

- During this stage, containers (small, cross-functional teams) are formed based on different aspects of the product, such as **feature sets** or **customer experiences**. Each container is responsible for exploring the unique challenges and opportunities within its domain.
- User research is conducted early, focusing on developing deep empathy for users. **Interviews, surveys**, and **observational research** help the teams understand their target audience. The findings are used to create detailed **user personas**, which reflect the specific needs and pain points of various user types.
- Teams use **empathy** as a core starting point. The focus is on understanding users' lives and the context in which they interact with your product. Cross-functional teams brainstorm and ideate creative solutions to the problems uncovered in the research. This exploration

phase allows teams to generate a broad range of potential ideas for solving the identified pain points.

- As the team enters the exploration stage, **mindfulness practices** can be introduced to ensure that team members remain present and focused.

Regular breaks, mindfulness exercises at the beginning of ideation sessions, and a supportive atmosphere help keep the team's energy balanced during this creative phase.

Scenario

For a SaaS platform designed to improve **remote team collaboration**, one container might be responsible for exploring **video conferencing** solutions. The team conducts in-depth interviews with remote workers and managers, discovering that many users experience **video fatigue** during long meetings. This insight drives the team to start thinking about innovative ways to make meetings more engaging and less tiring.

Phase 2: Define - Structuring Solutions

In the Define phase, the teams narrow their focus, using the insights gathered during the Explore phase to articulate the specific problems they aim to solve. Here, **structure** meets **creativity**, ensuring that teams can begin testing and iterating on their solutions

Actions:

- At this point, each container defines its objectives more clearly. The roles within the container become clearer, and each team creates **detailed objectives** and **success criteria** for the features, or user flows they are responsible for. Autonomy is granted, but teams remain aligned with the overall product strategy and vision.
- UCD principles continue to guide the development process. Teams take the research findings and create **user stories**, ensuring that every feature or solution being developed meets the specific needs and preferences of the users. Early **prototypes** are designed based on these user stories, often starting with wireframes or clickable mockups.
- The problem-definition phase of Design Thinking takes precedence here. Teams work to define the specific problem they're solving clearly. They might ask, "How can we make remote meetings more **engaging** while reducing **cognitive load**?" The team narrows

down ideas generated in the Explore phase, selecting the most viable ones to **prototype** and **test**.

- The Define phase can be intense, as teams must balance creative ideation with technical execution. **Mindful practices** help reduce stress and improve focus. For instance, start each workday with a brief mindfulness exercise or maintain **open, empathetic communication** within the team to ensure emotional well-being during high-pressure phases.

> **Scenario**
>
> In the Explore phase, the **task management** container may have discovered that users find it hard to prioritize tasks efficiently when working remotely. Using UCD principles, the team creates **user stories** like, "As a project manager, I need a simple way to prioritize tasks so that I can ensure my team stays focused on high-impact work." They then prototype a new task prioritization feature and begin testing it internally.

Phase 3: Evaluate - Refining and Iterating

The evaluation phase is where the integration of user feedback, continuous improvement, and mindful collaboration occurs. Teams gather data, iterate on their solutions, and ensure that the product is not only solving user problems but also evolving with their needs.

Actions:

- Containers evaluate their solutions based on feedback from real users. They conduct **testing cycles**, gathering user feedback and refining their prototypes. Each container adjusts its work to meet both user needs and performance goals.
- UCD remains central during evaluation, ensuring that the product evolves through real **user testing**. Usability tests and feedback sessions allow teams to refine their features based on how users interact with them. This iterative feedback loop ensures that the product stays relevant and continues solving real problems.
- Design Thinking's **testing and feedback** stages are vital during the evaluation process. Rapid **prototyping** and **user feedback** loops help teams refine their solutions continuously. Design Thinking encourages teams to test small iterations of their solution with real users, ensuring that each iteration moves closer to the best possible solution.

- As teams evaluate and iterate, mindfulness helps maintain a balanced approach to feedback. Whether the feedback is positive or negative, practicing **empathy** and **non-judgment** encourages constructive improvements and reduces frustration. Additionally, maintaining a **work-life balance** is critical during this phase to avoid burnout from constant iterations.

Scenario

For the **video conferencing** container, the team rolls out an early prototype of their **meeting engagement tools** to a small group of users. Feedback shows that while the features (such as quick icebreakers or fatigue-reduction timers) are valuable, users want more customization options. Based on this feedback, the team iterates on the design, refining the tool and running additional tests to ensure it delivers value.

The design container framework is A Cohesive, Iterative Approach to SaaS Product Development.

By integrating the **Container Method**, **User-Centered Design (UCD)**, **Design Thinking**, and **Mindfulness** under the **Explore**, **Define**, and **Evaluate** framework, teams can ensure that they build innovative, user-centered SaaS products while maintaining team well-being and resilience. This approach fosters creativity, keeps the product grounded in real user needs, and enables continuous improvement through mindful, focused collaboration.

- **Explore**: Teams build deep empathy, research user needs, and brainstorm solutions.
- **Define**: Teams structure their solutions, develop user stories, and start prototyping.
- **Evaluate**: Teams iterate based on feedback, refine solutions, and continue improving.

This holistic approach ensures a balance between innovation, user focus, and team health, leading to a successful and sustainable product development process.

Bonus Chapter

Sustainability in Software: Why and How to Incorporate Environmental Measures into Product Development

In an era where environmental concerns dominate global conversations, Software as a Service (SaaS) and enterprise technology companies are not exempt from their share of responsibility. As industries seek to decarbonize and reduce their environmental impact, the tech sector—which historically focuses on rapid growth, scalability, and efficiency—faces increasing pressure to embrace sustainability in their products and practices.

For software development and design teams, incorporating environmental measures in the product lifecycle is no longer optional. Regulatory bodies, stakeholders, customers, and even employees are demanding environmentally conscious solutions. This chapter explores **why** and **how** software companies, particularly SaaS and enterprise tech firms, need to take environmental sustainability seriously and integrate these measures into the development process.

Why Environmental Considerations Are Crucial

1. Growing Environmental Awareness and Market Demand

Today's customers and businesses are more environmentally aware than ever before. Many now prioritize products and services that minimize carbon footprints and actively seek companies that champion sustainability. The sustainability performance of a company can influence purchasing decisions, customer loyalty, and brand reputation. SaaS and enterprise tech companies, whose products are critical in powering entire industries, play a pivotal role in either contributing to or reducing environmental impacts.

2. Energy Consumption and Data Centers

The tech industry consumes an enormous amount of energy. Data centers, which are the backbone of SaaS products, require continuous power and cooling systems that have a significant carbon footprint. It is estimated that data centers contribute to around 1-2% of global energy consumption, a figure projected to rise dramatically without intervention. By designing more energy-efficient software, minimizing data storage needs, and optimizing cloud usage, companies can reduce these impacts.

3. Regulatory Pressures

Governments across the world are tightening regulations on energy use, electronic waste, and carbon emissions. Tech companies that fail to meet new compliance standards risk hefty fines, restrictions, and damage to their brand. The European Union's Green Deal and the United States' focus on climate policy are just a few examples of regions where sustainability regulations are becoming more stringent. Companies that proactively integrate environmental measures can stay ahead of regulatory changes and avoid the risk of non-compliance.

4. Investor and Stakeholder Expectations

Institutional investors are increasingly scrutinizing companies for their environmental, social, and governance (ESG) performance. Tech companies that lack a credible sustainability strategy risk losing investor confidence and capital. Investors are aware that a company's ability to manage environmental risks is directly tied to long-term profitability. As a result, incorporating environmental measures into software development helps mitigate risks, ensure business continuity, and enhance investor relations.

5. Talent Attraction and Retention

A growing number of software engineers and developers want to work for organizations that prioritize sustainability. According to recent surveys, top talent is attracted to companies that align with their values, particularly when it comes to environmental issues. SaaS companies that embed sustainability into their business practices not only attract a better workforce but also create a culture of responsibility that enhances employee engagement and retention.

How to Incorporate Environmental Measures in SaaS and Enterprise Tech

Now that the "why" is clear, the next question is **how** can SaaS and enterprise tech companies effectively integrate environmental considerations into the development of their products? Below are key strategies and actionable steps for design and software development teams.

1. Sustainable Product Design

Sustainable design is a critical starting point. Teams need to consider the environmental impact of their products at every stage of development. Some approaches include:

- **Optimizing Code for Efficiency**: Inefficient code consumes more computing power and, consequently, more energy. Designing software that runs faster and requires fewer resources helps reduce the overall energy footprint.
- **Modular and Scalable Designs**: By making software modular, companies can reduce redundant processes and hardware usage, allowing the product to scale efficiently without unnecessarily increasing resource consumption.
- **User Behavior Considerations**: Designing features that encourage users to minimize unnecessary data use or storage (e.g., encouraging deletion of outdated data, efficient use of processing power) can significantly reduce environmental impact.

2. Cloud Infrastructure Optimization

One of the largest contributors to energy use in SaaS applications is cloud computing. Optimizing cloud infrastructure is a key area where significant environmental benefits can be achieved:

- **Server Optimization**: Moving workloads to more energy-efficient cloud providers that use renewable energy can reduce emissions. Leading providers like AWS, Microsoft Azure, and Google Cloud have already made commitments to sustainable practices and offer options for carbon-efficient cloud computing.
- **Autoscaling and Elasticity**: Dynamic scaling of resources based on demand reduces wasted energy. Design systems that only use the resources required at any given time, reducing idle infrastructure.
- **Edge Computing**: By processing data closer to where it is generated, edge computing can reduce latency and energy costs associated with long-distance data transmission.

3. Energy-Efficient Data Storage

Reducing energy use in data storage is another important consideration:

- **Data Minimization**: Implement policies and designs that prioritize the minimization of stored data. For example, encourage customers to purge old or unnecessary data, and apply automatic data deletion processes for files that no longer need to be stored.
- **Data Compression**: Use efficient data compression algorithms to reduce the size of data being stored and transmitted, which in turn reduces energy consumption for storage and networking.
- **Green Data Centers**: Use data centers that employ renewable energy and optimize cooling systems, or use energy-efficient alternatives like liquid cooling to reduce environmental impact.

4. Lifecycle Assessment and Circularity

Performing a lifecycle assessment (LCA) helps companies evaluate the environmental impact of a product from the design phase through to its end of life. This can guide decisions on how to reduce waste, improve energy efficiency, and create a circular product lifecycle:

- **Design for Longevity**: Build software that can easily adapt to future requirements without becoming obsolete. Avoid creating software that relies on frequent updates, which can require the continuous use of additional resources.
- **End-of-Life Management**: If the software or hardware reaches an end-of-life stage, ensure that there are sustainable options for decommissioning and recycling to avoid contributing to electronic waste.

5. Cross-Departmental Collaboration

Environmental sustainability in software development requires close collaboration across various departments. Design teams need to work with data scientists, cloud infrastructure engineers, and business leaders to ensure that sustainability is part of the broader corporate strategy. Bringing in experts from fields like renewable energy, data efficiency, and circular design can help teams make more informed choices when building new products.

6. Environmental Impact Metrics and Reporting

SaaS companies should implement tracking and reporting mechanisms to measure the environmental impact of their software products. Some relevant metrics might include:

- **Energy consumption per transaction**
- **Carbon emissions associated with data storage and transmission**
- **Water usage in cooling for data centers**
- **Amount of e-waste generated**

Regularly reporting these metrics can help companies not only identify areas for improvement but also communicate their environmental performance to customers, investors, and regulatory bodies.

The environmental challenges facing the world today call for every industry, including technology, to adopt more sustainable practices.

For SaaS and enterprise tech companies, incorporating environmental measures into software design and development is not just a moral imperative; it is becoming **a competitive advantage and a regulatory necessity**.

By embracing energy-efficient design, optimizing cloud infrastructure, reducing data storage impacts, and fostering collaboration across departments, these companies can significantly **reduce their carbon footprint while enhancing business value.**

Sustainability is not just about reducing harm; it's about creating smarter, more responsible technology for the future.

Book Notes + Thoughts

www.ingramcontent.com/pod-product-compliance
Lightning Source LLC
Chambersburg PA
CBHW050307230526
45471CB00005B/2070